Educator's Playbook

The Teaching Learning toolkit

25 Proven Classroom strategies with Lesson Plans

By-Pooja Foria

About the author

Pooja Foria is an experienced educator with 16 years of dedication to teaching, mentoring, and inspiring learners. She has played a pivotal role in shaping students academically, socially, and personally, guided by her belief in preparing them not just for today but for the challenges of tomorrow through innovative teaching-learning practices. Her unique style lies in creating engaging lessons by blending strategies with simulations and creative activities.

Her first seven years of school teaching experience laid the foundation for her growth, helping her evolve into the accomplished educator, she is today. In recent years, she has expanded her role from teaching to consulting and guiding young minds in choosing the right paths, as well as training teachers to adopt innovative and creative methodologies.

In her eighteen years of career, she has been a strong advocate of teaching theoretical concepts through practical applications, integrating technical tools to stay relevant in an ever-evolving world. She believes resilience and adaptability are key, and she takes pride in empowering both students and teachers with unique, forward-thinking learning engagements. Her passion for sharing knowledge continues to inspire those around her.

Preface

Teaching is both an art and a science, a delicate balance between creativity and structure, inspiration and methodology. At its core, teaching is about igniting curiosity, fostering understanding, and empowering students to think critically and independently. It is a journey that requires patience, innovation, and the ability to adapt to the diverse needs of learners.

The strategies presented in this book aim to transform the way lessons are delivered, making teaching dynamic, engaging, and effective. These approaches are rooted in real classroom experiences and tested with students of different age groups and abilities. Whether you're a new teacher stepping into a classroom for the first time or a seasoned educator looking to refresh your practice, this toolkit offers something for everyone.

Each strategy is designed to address key challenges faced by educators, such as maintaining student attention, encouraging active participation, and ensuring concepts are understood and retained. You'll find practical, step-by-step methods paired with relatable examples that can be easily adapted across various subjects, from language arts to science, and even interdisciplinary projects.

The purpose of this book is not just to offer ideas but to inspire a mind-set of continuous improvement. Teaching is a profession that evolves with every lesson, every interaction, and every reflection. By embracing these strategies, educators can make their classrooms spaces of discovery, where learning feels exciting and meaningful.

Beyond methods, this book emphasizes the importance of planning and execution. While creativity and innovation are crucial, effective teaching also requires careful preparation and thoughtful implementation. Multi-tasking in a classroom can feel overwhelming, but with well-structured plans and clear objectives, it becomes manageable—and even enjoyable.

Acknowledgments

First and foremost, I express my deepest gratitude to God, whose grace and blessings have guided me through every step of this journey.

To my parents and family, your unwavering love and motivation have been the cornerstone of my achievements. Thank you for believing in me and encouraging me to follow my passion and whatever I select to do in my life when it comes to learning.

I extend heartfelt appreciation to my stalwart principals, whose wise words and vision have shaped me into the educator I am today. Your guidance and mentorship have been invaluable.

To the coordinators who meticulously explained each mistake and helped me refine my craft, thank you for your patience and commitment. Your support made every challenge a learning opportunity.

I am equally grateful to the mentors who inspired me through Impactful workshops and shared their expertise, enriching my journey with shared ideas.

This book is dedicated to my parents, mentors and educators around the globe from whom I received this vast knowledge and expertise and with pride and responsibility would love to share it with other teachers new or seasoned, parents and all those who love to teach. It encapsulates my journey of continually improving lessons to make them creative yet time-efficient. Each strategy was chosen for weaving and practicing varied approaches in classrooms, fostering excitement and engagement in students across various subjects.

As a founder, educational consultant, and mentor, I have seen first-hand how these ground-breaking strategies have brought chutzpah and joy to learning. I believe that planning with careful execution can transform lessons into experiences that students eagerly anticipate.

The 25 strategies and lesson plans shared in this book are a culmination of my learnings from my first day at work till now, and I hope they inspire you to craft exciting, impactful lessons. May this book serve as a guide to spark creativity and make a difference in your teaching journey.

With gratitude and hope,
Pooja Foria

Contents

Lesson Plan: The Water Cycle – Traffic signal strategy

Grade Level: 3–5
Duration: 60 minutes
Theme: Understanding the Water Cycle using traffic signal

Learning Objectives

By the end of the lesson, students will:

1. Understand the main processes of the water cycle (evaporation, condensation, precipitation, and collection).
2. Use inquiry to explore how the water cycle is a continuous process.
3. Engage in reflective thinking using the Traffic Signal Water Cycle strategy to self-assess and deepen their understanding.

Materials Needed

- A large diagram of the water cycle (poster or digital).
- Colored cards (red, yellow, green).
- Markers, chart paper, and sticky notes.
- Water, kettle (for steam demonstration), clear jar, ice cubes, and lamp (optional for hands-on activity).
- Worksheet with prompts for inquiry and observations.

Lesson Flow

1. Engage (10 minutes)

- **Warm-up Question**: Ask, "Have you ever wondered where the rain comes from or where it goes after it hits the ground?"
- Show a quick, engaging video/animation of the water cycle.
- Introduce the concept with a question: "What do you think happens to a puddle after it rains?"

2. Explore (15 minutes)

- **Hands-on Demonstration**:
    - Use a kettle to demonstrate evaporation. Explain how heat causes water to turn into steam.
    - Show condensation using a jar, hot water, and ice cubes to mimic cloud formation.
    - Discuss precipitation using visuals or letting water droplets fall from the jar lid.
- Split the students into small groups to create a mini water cycle in a bag (ziplock bag with water taped to a window for observation).
- Encourage students to make observations and note their questions during the activity.

3. Explain (10 minutes)

- Discuss the processes in the water cycle using a large diagram or interactive whiteboard. Highlight keywords: evaporation, condensation, precipitation, and collection.
- Link the hands-on activity to real-world phenomena like rain, rivers, and oceans.

4. Elaborate with Traffic Signal Water Cycle (20 minutes)

- **Strategy Introduction**:

- o   Provide each student with red, yellow, and green cards.
    - o   Green = "I understand this concept well."
    - o   Yellow = "I am somewhat clear but have some doubts."
    - o   Red = "I don't understand this concept yet."
- **Activity Steps**:
    1. Read or display a key question (e.g., "What happens to water after it evaporates?").
    2. Students use their cards to signal their understanding.
    3. Based on signals:
        - **Green**: Ask students to explain the concept in their own words or add examples.
        - **Yellow**: Prompt them with leading questions to clarify doubts.
        - **Red**: Revisit the topic with peer help or additional explanations.
- Rotate through several questions, gradually making them more analytical (e.g., "What would happen if evaporation stopped?").

5. Evaluate (5 minutes)

- Students complete a reflection worksheet:
    1. What is one thing you learned today?
    2. What is one question you still have?
    3. What was your favorite part of the lesson?
- Collect the worksheets to assess understanding and plan follow-up lessons.

Extensions

- **Art Connection**: Create a collaborative mural of the water cycle with labeled stages.

Lesson Plan: The Digestive System – Snowball strategy

Grade Level: 5–7
Duration: 60 minutes
Theme: Understanding the Digestive System using snow ball strategy

Learning Objectives

By the end of the lesson, students will:

1. Understand the major organs and functions of the digestive system.
2. Explore how food travels and is processed in the body.
3. Use the Snowball strategy to collaboratively learn and explain digestion.

Materials Needed

*   A labeled diagram of the digestive system (poster or digital).
*   Flashcards with facts about each organ in the digestive system.
*   Chart paper, sticky notes, and markers.
*   Worksheet with guided questions about the digestive system.

Lesson Flow

1. Engage (10 minutes)

*   **Warm-up Question**: Ask, "What happens to the food we eat?"

- Show a short animation or video clip illustrating the digestive system in action.
- Prompt discussion with, "If you eat an apple, where does it go? How does it turn into energy for your body?"

2. Explore (15 minutes)

- **Hands-on Activity**:
    - Show a labeled model or diagram of the digestive system.
    - Use analogies (e.g., "The stomach is like a blender that mixes food with juices to break it down").
    - Walk through the journey of food: mouth → esophagus → stomach → intestines → anus.
- **Group Activity**:
    - Divide the class into small groups.
    - Assign each group a specific part of the digestive system to explore. Provide flashcards with information about their assigned organ.

3. Explain (10 minutes)

- Have each group present their assigned organ's function to the class.
- Use a class diagram or interactive board to connect each group's explanation to create a complete journey of digestion.

4. Elaborate with Snowball Strategy (20 minutes)

- **Strategy Introduction:**

- o Start with a simple question for individual students to think about, e.g., "Why do we need digestion?"
  - o Students write their responses individually on a sheet of paper.
- **Activity Steps**:
  1. **Pair Sharing**: Students pair up, share their responses, and combine their ideas.
  2. **Small Group Sharing**: Pairs join another pair to form groups of four. They further discuss and refine their understanding.
  3. **Whole-Class Sharing**: Groups share their combined ideas with the entire class.
- During each stage, encourage students to focus on questions like:
  - o What are the key processes in digestion?
  - o Why is each organ important?
  - o What would happen if one part of the digestive system didn't work?

5. Evaluate (5 minutes)

- Students complete a short worksheet with reflective prompts:
  1. Name the main parts of the digestive system and their functions.
  2. What is one new thing you learned today?
  3. What is one question you still have about digestion?
- Collect the worksheets to assess understanding and note any misconceptions for follow-up lessons.

Extensions

- **Art Connection**: Create a labeled digestive system diagram as a class mural or use clay to make the organs.

13

- **Interactive Activity**: Conduct a digestion simulation using household items to represent stomach acid, bile, etc.

Lesson Plan: Simple Machines – Think-pair-share

Grade Level: 3–5
Duration: 60 minutes
Theme: Understanding Simple Machines using Think-pair-share strategy

Learning Objectives

By the end of the lesson, students will:

1. Identify and understand the six types of simple machines (lever, wheel and axle, pulley, inclined plane, screw, wedge).
2. Explore how simple machines make work easier.
3. Use the Think-Pair-Share strategy to analyze and explain how simple machines are used in everyday life.

Materials Needed

- Pictures or real-life examples of simple machines (scissors, ramp, screw, etc.).
- Chart paper and markers.
- A worksheet with guided questions.
- Flashcards with simple machine types and their descriptions.
- Optional: toy models of simple machines for hands-on exploration.

Lesson Flow

1. Engage (10 minutes)

- **Warm-up Question**: Ask, *"Have you ever used a tool or device that made a task easier? What was it?"*
- Show a short video or pictures of simple machines in action (e.g., seesaw, bicycle, pulley system).
- Prompt discussion with, *"What do you think these tools have in common? How do they help us?"*

2. Explore (15 minutes)

- **Hands-on Exploration**:
    - Display and describe examples of each simple machine.
    - Use physical examples like a lever (ruler and eraser as a fulcrum), inclined plane (board), and wheel and axle (toy car).
    - Discuss how these tools reduce effort and make work easier.
- **Group Activity**:
    - Divide students into six groups, each assigned a specific simple machine.
    - Provide flashcards with the machine's name, definition, and examples.
    - Groups explore their machine and prepare to explain its function to the class.

3. Explain (10 minutes)

- Groups present their simple machine, explaining:
    - Its name and how it works.
    - Real-life examples of where it is used.
    - How it makes work easier.
- Use a class chart or interactive board to categorize the six machines and connect their functions.

4. Elaborate with Think-Pair-Share Strategy (20 minutes)

- **Strategy Introduction**: Explain that students will think about a question, discuss it with a partner, and then share their ideas with the class.
- **Activity Steps**:
    1. **Think**: Pose a question like:
        - *"Which simple machine do you think is the most useful in everyday life and why?"*
        - *"How would life be different if simple machines didn't exist?"* Students individually write down their thoughts.
    2. **Pair**: Students pair up to discuss their answers and exchange ideas. Encourage them to ask each other questions like:
        - *Why did you choose that machine?*
        - *Can you think of another example where it's used?*
    3. **Share**: Pairs share their responses with the whole class.
        - Compile responses on the board, grouping similar ideas.
        - Highlight diverse examples and perspectives shared by students.

5. Evaluate (5 minutes)

- Students complete a reflection worksheet:
    1. Name three simple machines and an example of each.
    2. Which simple machine do you find most interesting and why?
    3. What is one question you still have about simple machines?
- Collect the worksheets to assess understanding and identify areas needing review.

Extensions

- **Engineering Challenge**: Have students build a compound machine (e.g., using Lego or recycled materials) that combines two or more simple machines.
- **Observation Task**: Ask students to identify simple machines in their home or playground and share their findings in the next class.
- **Math Connection**: Explore how simple machines reduce force using basic calculations (e.g., comparing effort required to lift weights with and without a pulley).

Lesson Plan: The Circulatory System – Brainstorm Blast strategy

Grade Level: 4–6
Duration: 60 minutes
Theme: Exploring the Circulatory System using Brainstorm blast strategy

Learning Objectives

By the end of the lesson, students will:

1. Identify the main components of the circulatory system (heart, blood, blood vessels).
2. Understand the function of the circulatory system in transporting oxygen, nutrients, and waste.
3. Use the Brainstorm Blast strategy to generate and share ideas about how the circulatory system works.

Materials Needed
- Diagram of the circulatory system (poster or digital).
- Flashcards with circulatory system facts and vocabulary (e.g., heart, arteries, veins, capillaries).
- Sticky notes, markers, and chart paper.
- A stopwatch or timer.
- Balloons (optional for hands-on demonstration).
- Worksheet with reflective questions.

Lesson Flow

1. Engage (10 minutes)

- **Warm-up Question**: Ask, "What do you think happens inside your body when you run or jump?"

- Show a short video or animation about the circulatory system.
- Prompt discussion with, "Why is blood important? How does it move through your body?"
- Take quick initial responses and note common ideas on the board.

2. Explore (15 minutes)

- **Hands-on Demonstration**:
  - Use a balloon pump to mimic the heart pumping blood. Squeeze and release to show how blood is pushed through the blood vessels.
  - Show a diagram of the circulatory system, explaining the roles of the heart, arteries, veins, and capillaries.
- **Small Group Exploration**:
  - Divide the class into three groups.
    - Group 1: Explore the heart and its pumping action.
    - Group 2: Explore arteries, veins, and capillaries.
    - Group 3: Explore the role of blood in transporting oxygen and nutrients.
  - Provide each group with flashcards or models related to their topic.
  - Groups discuss their topic and prepare to share one key fact with the class.

3. Explain (10 minutes)

- Groups present their findings to the class.
- Use an interactive board or poster to connect the pieces into a complete explanation of the circulatory system.

- Highlight how oxygenated blood travels from the heart to the body and how deoxygenated blood returns to the heart.

4. Elaborate with Brainstorm Blast Strategy (20 minutes)

- **Strategy Introduction**: Explain that the class will brainstorm ideas in short bursts of time.
- **Activity Steps**:
    1. **Prompt**: Pose a series of questions to the class, one at a time:
        - "Why do we need a circulatory system?"
        - "What would happen if blood stopped circulating?"
        - "How can we keep our circulatory system healthy?"
    2. **Blast Phase**:
        - Set a timer for 1 minute for each question.
        - Students quickly write or shout out as many ideas as they can.
        - Record responses on chart paper or sticky notes.
    3. **Discuss and Categorize**:
        - Group similar ideas and highlight key points.
        - Use follow-up questions to clarify or expand on students' ideas.

5. Evaluate (5 minutes)

- Students complete a reflection worksheet with questions like:
    1. Name the main parts of the circulatory system.
    2. Why is the heart important?

3. What is one way you can take care of your heart and blood vessels?

- Collect worksheets to assess understanding and identify areas for review.

Extensions

- **STEM Challenge**: Create a simple model of the circulatory system using straws (as blood vessels), a sponge (as the heart), and water (as blood).
- **Health Connection**: Discuss the importance of exercise and healthy eating for a strong circulatory system.
- **Technology Integration**: Use an interactive simulation or app to explore how the heart pumps blood.

Lesson Plan: Writing Informal Letters – Round Robin Strategy

Grade Level: 3–5
Duration: 60 minutes
Theme: <u>Understanding and Practicing Informal Letter Writing using Round Robin Strategy</u>

Learning Objectives

By the end of the lesson, students will:

1. Identify the structure and key elements of an informal letter (sender's address, date, salutation, body, closing, and signature).
2. Understand the purpose and tone of informal letters.
3. Use the Round Robin strategy to collaboratively draft and refine an informal letter.

Materials Needed

- Examples of informal letters (printed or projected).
- Chart paper and markers.
- Writing paper or notebooks.
- Worksheet with prompts and an outline for informal letters.

Lesson Flow

1. Engage (10 minutes)

- **Warm-up Question**: Ask, "When was the last time you wrote a letter or sent a message to a friend or family member? What did you write about?"

- Show an example of an informal letter. Read it aloud and ask students:
  - "Who do you think the letter is addressed to?"
  - "What is the writer's purpose?"
- Highlight the friendly and conversational tone of informal letters.

2. Explore (15 minutes)

- **Parts of an Informal Letter**:
  - Use a chart or projector to explain the structure:
    1. Sender's address
    2. Date
    3. Salutation (e.g., Dear [Name])
    4. Body (main message)
    5. Closing (e.g., Yours sincerely, With love)
    6. Signature
- **Group Activity**:
  - Divide students into small groups.
  - Provide each group with an example of an incomplete informal letter.
  - Ask them to identify and label its parts.

3. Explain (10 minutes)

- Discuss the tone and content of an informal letter, emphasizing that it should feel like a conversation.
- Provide writing prompts to inspire ideas (e.g., Write a letter to a friend about your holiday trip or Write to your cousin inviting them to your birthday party).

4. Elaborate with Round Robin Strategy (20 minutes)

- **Strategy Introduction**: Explain that students will work in small groups to collaboratively draft a letter using the Round Robin strategy.
- **Activity Steps**:
  1. **Start the Letter**:
     - Each group is assigned a writing prompt.
     - One student in each group starts by writing the sender's address and date.
  2. **Pass and Add**:
     - The paper is passed to the next student, who adds the salutation and starts the body of the letter.
     - Each subsequent student adds a sentence or detail to the letter, ensuring it stays on topic and follows the informal tone.
  3. **Finalize**:
     - The last student adds the closing and signature.
- **Sharing and Feedback**:
  - Groups read their letters aloud.
  - Discuss what was done well and how the letters could be improved.

5. Evaluate (5 minutes)

- Students complete a short reflection worksheet:
  1. Name two important parts of an informal letter.
  2. What is one thing you enjoyed about writing the letter?
  3. What is one thing you found challenging?
- Collect the worksheets and group letters for assessment.

Extensions

- **Individual Practice**: Students write an informal letter to a family member or friend as homework.
- **Art Connection**: Create decorated envelopes for their letters.
- **Technology Integration**: Introduce email writing as a modern form of informal letter writing.

Lesson Plan: Understanding Ancient Civilizations – Jigsaw learning

Grade Level: 5–7
Duration: 60 minutes
Theme: Understanding Ancient Civilizations using Jigsaw learning

Learning Objectives:

By the end of the lesson, students will be able to:

1. Identify key characteristics of ancient civilizations (e.g., Mesopotamia, Egypt, Indus Valley, and China).
2. Compare and contrast cultural, political, and economic aspects of these civilizations.
3. Collaboratively share information through a jigsaw activity.
4. Draw conclusions about the contributions of ancient civilizations to modern society.

Materials Needed:

- Chart papers, markers, and handouts
- Pre-assigned reading materials for each civilization
- A worksheet with guiding questions for students

Lesson Flow:

1. Engagement (10 minutes)
Activity: Class Discussion and Inquiry Prompt

- Begin by asking:

27

- What do you think life was like in ancient times?
- What do you already know about ancient civilizations?
- Why do you think learning about ancient civilizations is important today?

- Write responses on the board to build excitement and generate questions.

Transition to Exploration: Tell students they will become "experts" on one civilization and then teach others about it.

2. Exploration (20 minutes)
Activity: Jigsaw Learning in Expert Groups

1. **Divide the class** into 4 groups, each assigned one ancient civilization:
   - Group 1: Mesopotamia
   - Group 2: Ancient Egypt
   - Group 3: Indus Valley
   - Group 4: Ancient China
2. **Provide materials** (e.g., short readings, images, maps) tailored to each group's topic.
3. Students work together in their expert groups to answer the following guiding questions:
   - Where was this civilization located?
   - What were their key cultural, technological, or political achievements?
   - How did their geography influence their development?
   - What is one lasting legacy of this civilization?

3. Explanation (15 minutes)
Activity: Sharing Knowledge in Home Groups

1. Regroup students into **home groups** consisting of one representative from each expert group.
2. Each "expert" teaches their peers about their assigned civilization, using visual aids or notes created in the expert group.
3. Peers complete a comparison chart during the sharing process.

4. Elaboration (10 minutes)
Activity: Class Synthesis

- Reconvene as a whole class to compare findings.
- Prompt questions such as:
    - What similarities and differences did you notice?
    - How did geography shape each civilization's development?
    - Which contribution from an ancient civilization do we still see today?
- Create a collaborative timeline or map showcasing all civilizations.

5. Evaluation (5 minutes)
Activity: Reflective Assessment

- Distribute a short reflective worksheet or have student's journal about:
    - What did you find most interesting about ancient civilizations?
    - What skills did you practice in today's activity?

Adaptations for Diverse Learners:

- Use videos or interactive online tools for students who need visual aids.

- Provide simplified readings or a buddy system for struggling readers.
- Encourage advanced learners to research an additional civilization or topic of their choice.

Homework Extension:

Students create a poster or a short paragraph about their favorite ancient civilization, highlighting its contributions to modern life.

Lesson Plan: Understanding Rights and Responsibilities – Concept mapping

Grade Level: 3–5
Duration: 60 minutes
Theme: <u>Understanding Rights and responsibilities using concept mapping.</u>

Learning Objectives:

By the end of the lesson, students will be able to:

1. Define and differentiate between rights and responsibilities.
2. Identify examples of rights and responsibilities at home, school, and community levels.
3. Create a concept map that visually organizes the relationship between rights and responsibilities.
4. Reflect on how fulfilling responsibilities helps protect rights.

Materials Needed:

- Chart papers, markers, sticky notes
- Handouts with scenarios involving rights and responsibilities
- Example concept map template (for guidance)
- Guiding questions worksheet

Lesson Flow:

1. Engagement (10 minutes)
Activity: Class Brainstorm and Inquiry Prompt

- Write "Rights" and "Responsibilities" on the board.
- Ask students:
  - What does the word "rights" mean to you?
  - What does "responsibilities" mean?
  - Can you think of examples of rights and responsibilities in your daily life?
- Create two lists based on their responses, leaving room for additions later.
- Pose the essential inquiry question:
  - Why do we need both rights and responsibilities in a community?

2. Exploration (15 minutes)
Activity: Group Work on Scenarios

1. Divide students into small groups and give each group a scenario (e.g., a student helping keep the classroom clean, a family member voting, or a child sharing toys with siblings).
2. Each group discusses:
   - What rights are involved in the scenario?
   - What responsibilities go along with those rights?
3. Groups record their answers on sticky notes: one color for rights and another for responsibilities.

3. Explanation (15 minutes)
Activity: Creating a Concept Map

1. Explain how concept mapping works: Start with a central idea and branch out to related concepts.
2. On a large chart paper or whiteboard, draw an example concept map with the central idea: "Rights and Responsibilities." Add sample branches such as:
   - At School
   - At Home
   - In the Community

3. Groups create their own concept maps using their sticky notes from the exploration activity. They can organize their examples under broader categories or themes.

4. Elaboration (15 minutes)
Activity: Class Discussion and Refinement

- Groups present their concept maps to the class.
- Facilitate a discussion to compare and refine the maps by asking:
    - Did any rights or responsibilities appear in multiple groups? Why do you think that is?
    - How do responsibilities help protect rights?
    - What happens when people ignore their responsibilities?
- Work as a class to create a combined concept map that incorporates everyone's ideas.

5. Evaluation (5 minutes)
Activity: Reflection and Exit Ticket

- Students write or share orally:
    - One right that is important to you and the responsibility that goes with it.
    - One thing you learned about how rights and responsibilities are connected.

Adaptations for Diverse Learners:

- Provide visual aids (pictures, symbols) for students who need extra support.
- Allow advanced learners to add branches to their maps, such as "Global Rights and Responsibilities."
- Offer sentence starters for students who need help articulating their ideas.

Homework Extension:

Students interview a family member about a right and responsibility they value in their community. They can bring back their findings to share with the class.

Lesson Plan: Exploring Heroes and Leaders – Role-play and Simulation

Grade Level: 3–5
Duration: 60 minutes
Theme: <u>Understanding about heroes and leaders using Role-play and Simulation</u>

Learning Objectives:

By the end of the lesson, students will be able to:

1. Identify characteristics of heroes and leaders.
2. Differentiate between a hero and a leader and recognize overlaps between the two.
3. Analyze the actions and decisions of historical and contemporary figures.
4. Participate in a roleplay or simulation to demonstrate an understanding of leadership and heroism.

Materials Needed:

- Character cards with brief descriptions of heroes and leaders (e.g., Mahatma Gandhi, Malala Yousafzai, Martin Luther King Jr., Florence Nightingale, etc.).
- Props for roleplay (e.g., hats, sashes, or simple symbols of leadership roles).
- Scenario cards for the simulation activity.
- Chart paper and markers for brainstorming.
- Reflection worksheets.

Lesson Flow:

1. Engagement (10 minutes)
Activity: Discussion and Inquiry Prompt

- Ask students:
    - Who is your hero? Why do you admire them?
    - What makes someone a leader? Can a leader also be a hero?
- Facilitate a brief discussion to list characteristics of heroes (e.g., brave, selfless) and leaders (e.g., inspiring, decisive) on the board.
- Introduce the inquiry question:
    - What qualities make someone a hero or a leader, and how do their actions impact others?

2. Exploration (15 minutes)
Activity: Role Assignment and Research

1. Divide students into small groups and assign each group a historical or contemporary figure (e.g., Abraham Lincoln, Harriet Tubman, Nelson Mandela).
2. Provide a character card and a short handout with key facts about the figure's life, achievements, and challenges.
3. Groups read about their assigned figure and answer guiding questions:
    - What challenges did this person face?
    - What actions made them a hero, leader, or both?
    - How did their actions impact others?

3. Explanation (15 minutes)
Activity: Roleplay

1. Each group prepares a short roleplay/skit based on a significant moment in their figure's life.

o   Example: Harriet Tubman leading a group to freedom, Gandhi organizing a peaceful protest, or Malala Yousafzai advocating for education.
2. Groups perform their roleplays for the class.
3. After each performance, engage in a quick debrief:
    o   What qualities of heroism or leadership did you observe?
    o   How did their actions inspire or help others?

4. Elaboration (15 minutes)
Activity: Simulation – Decision-Making as Leaders

1. Present students with a scenario that requires them to act as leaders making tough decisions.
    o   Scenario Example: You are a group of community leaders during a flood. Resources are limited, and you must decide how to allocate them to help the most people.
2. Each group discusses the scenario and presents their decisions, explaining the reasoning behind their choices.
3. As a class, discuss:
    o   What challenges did you face as a leader?
    o   How did you balance the needs of others with available resources?

5. Evaluation (5 minutes)
Activity: Reflection and Exit Ticket

- Students complete a short worksheet or journal entry reflecting on:
    o   One quality they admire in a hero or leader they learned about today.

- A situation where they showed leadership or heroism in their own lives.

Adaptations for Diverse Learners:

- Simplify character cards or provide visual aids for students who need additional support.
- Allow advanced learners to research and roleplay additional figures not provided.
- Provide sentence starters or graphic organizers for students who need assistance in expressing their ideas.

Homework Extension:

Students research and write a short paragraph about a local hero or leader in their community and present their findings in the next class.

Lesson Plan: Exploring Landforms and Water Bodies – Gallery walk

Grade Level: 1–3
Duration: 60 minutes
Theme: <u>Understanding exploring landforms and water using Gallery walk</u>

Learning Objectives:

By the end of the lesson, students will be able to:

1. Identify and describe different types of landforms and water bodies (e.g., mountains, rivers, lakes, oceans, etc.).
2. Understand how landforms and water bodies affect human life and the environment.
3. Collaboratively share their knowledge through a gallery walk activity.
4. Ask and answer questions related to landforms and water bodies during the walk.

Materials Needed:

- Large poster boards or chart paper
- Markers, crayons, and colored pencils
- Pre-prepared images and descriptions of various landforms and water bodies (printed or drawn on chart paper)
- Sticky notes or index cards for questions and comments
- Guide sheets with key questions for the gallery walk activity

Lesson Flow:

1. Engagement (10 minutes)
Activity: Introduction and Inquiry Prompt

- Begin by asking students:
    - What do you think a landform is?
    - Can you name any landforms or water bodies you have seen or learned about?
- Write the students' responses on the board.
- Introduce the inquiry question:
    - How do landforms and water bodies affect where people live and how they use the environment?
- Briefly explain what the class will be doing in the gallery walk: moving around to explore different landforms and water bodies, asking questions, and sharing thoughts.

2. Exploration (15 minutes)
Activity: Gallery Walk Preparation

1. Arrange the room so that each station displays information about a different landform or water body (e.g., mountains, rivers, lakes, oceans, deserts, valleys, seas, etc.).
2. At each station, provide a large poster or chart with:
    - A description of the landform or water body
    - Pictures or diagrams showing the landform or water body
    - Key facts about how the landform or water body affects the environment and people living near it
3. Divide students into small groups and assign each group a starting station.

3. Explanation (15 minutes)
Activity: Gallery Walk

1. Students walk around the room in their groups, spending 2-3 minutes at each station. At each station, students:
    o Read or discuss the information provided
    o Write down one question or comment about the landform or water body on a sticky note or index card
    o Look at the pictures or diagrams to help them visualize the landform or water body
2. After 2-3 minutes, groups rotate to the next station.

4. Elaboration (10 minutes)
Activity: Group Reflection and Discussion

1. Once all groups have visited each station, bring the class together for a discussion.
2. Ask the following questions to guide reflection:
    o What did you learn about how people adapt to different landforms and water bodies?
    o Which landform or water body would be the most challenging to live near and why?
    o How do you think landforms and water bodies influence where people build their cities?
3. Encourage students to ask questions based on the sticky notes or index cards they collected during the gallery walk.

5. Evaluation (5 minutes)
Activity: Exit Ticket or Reflection Worksheet

- Students reflect on what they learned by completing a short worksheet or exit ticket:
    o What is one new landform or water body you learned about today?
    o How do landforms and water bodies help or hinder human life?

Adaptations for Diverse Learners:

- Provide visual aids and simplified descriptions for students who need extra support.
- Allow advanced learners to explore additional landforms or water bodies beyond the provided stations.
- Use a buddy system for students who may need help moving around or understanding the material.

Homework Extension:

Students create a "Landform and Water Body" booklet, where they select their favorite landform or water body and write or draw about it. They can include a brief description, the impact on people, and how it's used by humans.

Lesson Plan: Environmental Conservation - Six Thinking Hats Strategy

Grade Level: 7–9
Duration: 60 minutes
Theme: Understanding Environmental conservation using Six Thinking hats.

Learning Objectives:

By the end of the lesson, students will be able to:

1. Understand the importance of environmental conservation.
2. Use the Six Thinking Hats strategy to explore different perspectives on environmental issues.
3. Collaboratively think critically about solutions for environmental conservation.
4. Develop a plan for how to help conserve the environment in their community.

Materials Needed:

- Six colored hats (real or symbolic, e.g., paper hats or colored headbands)
- Large poster or chart paper
- Markers or colored pencils
- Handouts with scenarios related to environmental conservation (e.g., pollution, deforestation, endangered species, recycling)
- Six Thinking Hats prompts or questions (listed below)
- Reflection sheets

Lesson Flow:

1. Engagement (10 minutes)
Activity: Introduction and Inquiry Prompt

- Begin by asking:
    - What does "environmental conservation" mean?
    - Why is it important to take care of our planet?
    - What are some things we can do to help protect the environment?
- Introduce the inquiry question:
    - How can we think about environmental issues from different perspectives to come up with solutions?
- Explain that students will use the **Six Thinking Hats** strategy to look at environmental conservation in different ways.

2. Exploration (15 minutes)
Activity: Introduction to Six Thinking Hats

1. **Introduce the Six Thinking Hats:**
    - **White Hat**: Focuses on facts and information. What do we know about environmental conservation?
    - **Red Hat**: Focuses on feelings and emotions. How does environmental conservation make us feel?
    - **Black Hat**: Focuses on caution and critical thinking. What are some problems or risks with environmental conservation efforts?
    - **Yellow Hat**: Focuses on positive thinking. What are the benefits of conserving the environment?

o **Green Hat**: Focuses on creativity and new ideas. How can we come up with new solutions for conservation?
   o **Blue Hat**: Focuses on organization and process. How will we organize our thinking and make decisions?

2. **Assign a Hat to Each Group:** Divide students into 6 small groups, each representing one of the thinking hats.
3. **Provide scenarios** related to environmental conservation, such as:
   o Reducing plastic waste
   o Protecting endangered species
   o Preventing deforestation
   o Promoting recycling and waste management

3. Explanation (15 minutes)
Activity: Group Discussions

1. Each group discusses the environmental conservation scenario from the perspective of their assigned hat.
   o **White Hat** (Facts): Discuss the scientific facts related to the conservation issue.
   o **Red Hat** (Feelings): Express how the conservation issue makes them feel.
   o **Black Hat** (Critical Thinking): Identify problems or challenges that could arise in trying to solve the environmental issue.
   o **Yellow Hat** (Positive Thinking): Think of the positive outcomes of solving the environmental issue.
   o **Green Hat** (Creativity): Brainstorm new, creative solutions to the environmental issue.

- o **Blue Hat** (Process): Organize the ideas from all groups and figure out how the class will move forward.

4. Elaboration (10 minutes)
Activity: Sharing and Building Consensus

1. Each group presents their findings and ideas based on their hat's perspective.
2. After all groups have presented, facilitate a whole-class discussion:
    - o What solutions seem the most practical?
    - o What challenges do we need to overcome to help conserve the environment?
    - o How can we combine different perspectives to come up with a comprehensive solution?
3. Create a collective action plan for environmental conservation that includes ideas from all six thinking hats. This could include simple actions like recycling programs, tree planting, reducing plastic use, etc.

5. Evaluation (5 minutes)
Activity: Reflection and Exit Ticket

- Distribute reflection sheets with the following prompts:
    - o What did you learn about environmental conservation?
    - o What new idea or solution did you come up with today that could help conserve the environment?
    - o How can you contribute to environmental conservation in your daily life?

Adaptations for Diverse Learners:

- Use visual aids or videos to explain the Six Thinking Hats strategy for students who need additional support.
- Allow students to work in pairs or small groups for more collaboration if they have difficulty with the discussion.
- Provide sentence starters or written prompts for students who need help organizing their thoughts.

Homework Extension:

Ask students to observe and write about an environmental conservation issue in their local community (e.g., littering, water usage, energy conservation). They should apply the Six Thinking Hats strategy to propose solutions and bring their findings back to class.

Lesson Plan: Understanding the Causes and Effects of Water Pollution - The Fishbowl Discussion

Grade Level: 2–4
Duration: 60 minutes
Theme: Understanding the Causes and Effects of Water Pollution using The Fishbowl Discussion

Learning Objectives:

By the end of the lesson, students will be able to:

1. Identify the main causes and effects of water pollution.
2. Analyze how human activities contribute to water pollution and its impact on the environment.
3. Participate in a structured Fishbowl discussion to explore different viewpoints on water pollution.
4. Propose possible solutions to reduce water pollution in their community.

Materials Needed:

- A set of prepared cards or posters with different causes and effects of water pollution (e.g., industrial waste, agricultural runoff, plastic waste, oil spills, etc.)
- Chart paper and markers for recording discussion points
- Fishbowl setup (chairs arranged in an inner circle for discussion and an outer circle for observers)
- Reflection worksheets or exit tickets
- Optional: Short video or image set on water pollution

Lesson Flow:

1. Engagement (10 minutes)
Activity: Introduction to Water Pollution and Inquiry Prompt

- Start by asking:
    - What do you think happens when water gets polluted?
    - Where have you seen pollution in water sources like rivers, lakes, or oceans?
    - Why is clean water important for humans and animals?
- Record responses on the board and highlight key points about water pollution.
- Pose the essential inquiry question:
    - How does water pollution affect the environment, and what can we do to stop it?

2. Exploration (15 minutes)
Activity: Research and Group Work

1. Divide students into small groups (3–4 students per group).
2. Give each group a set of cards or posters that describe different causes or effects of water pollution (e.g., agricultural runoff, plastic waste, harmful chemicals, death of aquatic animals, etc.).
3. Ask each group to read their assigned causes or effects and discuss:
    - How does this cause pollution?
    - What are the immediate and long-term effects of this kind of pollution?
4. Have each group prepare a brief explanation of their cause or effect to share with the class.

3. Explanation (15 minutes)
Activity: Fishbowl Discussion

1. Set up the classroom with two circles of chairs: an inner circle (Fishbowl) for the discussion and an outer circle for observing.
2. **Inner Circle Discussion (Fishbowl)**: Choose 4-6 students to sit in the inner circle. These students will engage in a structured discussion on the causes and effects of water pollution based on their group's research.
    - Encourage students in the inner circle to use their research to explain how water gets polluted and the consequences of it.
    - Ensure they reference real-world examples, such as oil spills, plastic waste, or chemical runoff.
3. **Outer Circle (Observers)**: The students in the outer circle observe the discussion, take notes, and think about questions or comments they want to share.

4. Elaboration (10 minutes)
Activity: Rotation and Reflection

1. After 5–7 minutes, have the groups in the outer circle rotate into the inner circle and continue the discussion.
2. While the new students in the inner circle discuss, the previous group (now in the outer circle) records key points and reflections.
3. After another 5–7 minutes, rotate again so that all students have a chance to participate in the Fishbowl discussion.
4. As a class, summarize the causes and effects of water pollution, noting any solutions proposed during the discussion.

5. Evaluation (5 minutes)
Activity: Reflection and Exit Ticket

- Students complete a short reflection worksheet or exit ticket with these prompts:
    - What is one cause of water pollution that surprised you?
    - How can we reduce water pollution in our community?
    - What was one solution discussed that you think could make a big difference?

Adaptations for Diverse Learners:

- Provide visual aids, such as pictures or videos showing examples of water pollution, to help students better understand the concepts.
- Allow advanced learners to research additional causes or effects of water pollution to add to the Fishbowl discussion.
- Use sentence starters or graphic organizers to help struggling students frame their ideas during the discussion.

Homework Extension:

Ask students to create a poster or digital presentation on a specific type of water pollution (e.g., plastic waste or agricultural runoff). They should explain its cause, effects, and one solution to reduce it.

Lesson Plan: Weather and Climate - The Four Corners Debate Strategy

Grade Level: 3–5
Duration: 60 minutes
Theme: <u>Understanding the weather and climate using the four corners debate strategy.</u>

Learning Objectives:

By the end of the lesson, students will be able to:

1. Understand the difference between weather and climate.
2. Discuss how weather and climate affect the environment and daily life.
3. Use the Four Corners Debate strategy to explore different perspectives on how human activities impact weather and climate.
4. Develop a reasoned argument based on scientific evidence during the debate.

Materials Needed:

- Four labeled corners in the classroom (or four designated areas in the room for debate positions)
- Prepared statements about weather, climate, and human activities (e.g., "Human activities cause climate change," "Weather is more predictable than climate," "Climate is more important than weather," "Weather is affected by human actions")
- Large poster or chart paper for recording key points from the debate
- Markers or colored pencils for student notes
- Reflection worksheets or exit tickets

Lesson Flow:

1. Engagement (10 minutes)

Activity: Introduction to Weather and Climate

- Begin by asking:
    - What is the difference between weather and climate?
    - Can you think of some examples of different types of weather?
    - What does climate mean, and how does it affect the world around us?
- Write responses on the board and summarize:
    - **Weather**: Day-to-day changes in atmospheric conditions (e.g., sunny, rainy, cloudy).
    - **Climate**: Long-term patterns and trends in temperature, humidity, and precipitation in a region.
- Pose the inquiry question:
    - How do weather and climate impact our lives and the environment?

2. Exploration (15 minutes)

Activity: Introduction to the Four Corners Debate Strategy

1. Explain the **Four Corners Debate** strategy:
    - The class will be given statements about weather, climate, and human activities.
    - Each corner of the room represents a different opinion:
        - **Corner 1**: Strongly Agree
        - **Corner 2**: Agree
        - **Corner 3**: Disagree
        - **Corner 4**: Strongly Disagree
    - Students must choose the corner that best represents their opinion on each statement

and be ready to explain why they hold that opinion.
2. Review the following debate statements (you can add or adjust these to fit your lesson):
   o Human activities cause climate change.
   o Weather is more predictable than climate.
   o Climate is more important than weather.
   o Weather is affected by human actions.

3. Explanation (15 minutes)
Activity: Four Corners Debate

1. Read the first statement aloud:
   o Human activities cause climate change.
2. Give students 30 seconds to move to the corner of the room that aligns with their opinion.
3. Once students have chosen a corner, ask representatives from each corner to explain their reasoning:
   o **Corner 1 (Strongly Agree):** "Why do you think human activities cause climate change?"
   o **Corner 2 (Agree):** "Why do you agree, but not strongly?"
   o **Corner 3 (Disagree):** "What makes you disagree with this statement?"
   o **Corner 4 (Strongly Disagree):** "Why do you strongly disagree with the statement?"
4. After each debate, discuss key points raised by the students and summarize their arguments on a chart or board.
5. Repeat the debate for each of the other statements, encouraging students to switch corners if their opinions change based on the discussion.

4. Elaboration (10 minutes)
Activity: Reflection and Group Discussion

1. After completing the Four Corners Debate, ask students to reflect on the different perspectives shared.
2. Facilitate a whole-class discussion with these questions:
    - How did your opinion change during the debate?
    - What new information or viewpoints did you learn?
    - Why is it important to understand the difference between weather and climate?
3. Ask students to consider how weather and climate affect their lives, such as through the clothes they wear, the food they grow, or how they prepare for weather events.

5. Evaluation (5 minutes)
Activity: Exit Ticket or Reflection Worksheet

- Students complete an exit ticket or short reflection worksheet:
    - What is one new thing you learned about the difference between weather and climate?
    - How can human activities impact weather and climate?
    - Which perspective from the Four Corners Debate did you agree with the most, and why?

Adaptations for Diverse Learners:

- Provide visual aids (e.g., weather vs. climate charts) to help students better understand the concepts.

- Offer sentence starters for students who need help expressing their opinions during the debate.
- Allow students to work in pairs to discuss the statements before moving to the debate.

Homework Extension:

Ask students to research a specific climate or weather event in history (e.g., a major hurricane or drought) and write a brief report on how it was impacted by human activities or natural processes.

Lesson Plan: Exploring Energy Sources Using Problem-Based Learning (PBL)

Grade Level: 4–6
Duration: 60 minutes
Theme: <u>Understanding the energy sources using the problem based learning.</u>

Learning Objectives:

By the end of the lesson, students will be able to:

1. Identify different types of energy sources (renewable and nonrenewable).
2. Understand how energy sources are used in daily life and their impact on the environment.
3. Apply problem-solving skills to explore ways to conserve energy and shift towards more sustainable energy sources.
4. Collaborate to design a solution to a real-world energy problem.

Materials Needed:

- Chart paper and markers
- Pre-prepared scenario cards describing real-world energy problems (e.g., an energy shortage, pollution from nonrenewable energy sources)
- Access to computers/tablets for research (optional)
- A list of different energy sources (renewable: solar, wind, hydro, geothermal, etc.; nonrenewable: coal, oil, natural gas, etc.)
- Whiteboard or smartboard for brainstorming solutions
- Problem-based learning (PBL) worksheets or reflection sheets

Lesson Flow:

1. Engagement (10 minutes)
Activity: Introduction to Energy Sources

- Begin with an open discussion:
    - What are some ways we use energy in our everyday lives?
    - What do you think "renewable" and "nonrenewable" energy mean?
    - Where does the energy we use come from?
- Write students' responses on the board and categorize them into "renewable" and "nonrenewable" energy sources.
- Introduce the inquiry question:
    - How can we find solutions to problems related to energy use and make our world more sustainable?

2. Exploration (15 minutes)
Activity: Introduction to Problem-Based Learning

1. **Present the Problem:**
    - Share the following scenario with the students:
        - Your community is experiencing frequent power outages due to energy shortages, and there's increasing pollution from nonrenewable energy sources. Your task is to design a plan to solve this problem by exploring alternative energy sources, reducing energy consumption, and finding ways to make the community more sustainable.

2. **Research and Brainstorming:**
    - Divide students into small groups (3–4 students per group).
    - Give each group a set of cards with information about different energy sources (renewable and nonrenewable).
    - Ask students to research (or review) the pros and cons of each energy source and its potential for solving the problem. Groups should also brainstorm ways to reduce energy consumption and use cleaner energy sources in their community.

3. Explanation (15 minutes)

Activity: Presenting Group Solutions

1. Have each group discuss their findings and create a simple action plan or proposal to address the energy problem. Their plan should include:
   - A summary of the energy sources they recommend for the community.
   - A detailed explanation of why they chose those energy sources (e.g., environmental impact, sustainability, cost, feasibility).
   - Ideas for reducing energy use or conserving energy in everyday life.
2. Groups present their solutions to the class. After each presentation, encourage the class to ask questions or offer feedback.

4. Elaboration (10 minutes)

Activity: Collaborative Discussion and Reflection

1. After all groups have presented, facilitate a class discussion:

- o   Which energy sources seem most suitable for your community? Why?
- o   How can we convince people in the community to switch to more sustainable energy sources?
- o   What are some challenges we might face in trying to use renewable energy sources, and how can we overcome them?

2. Record key points on the whiteboard or smartboard. Discuss how each proposed solution might work in the real world and its potential impact on the environment.

5. Evaluation (5 minutes)
Activity: Reflection Worksheet or Exit Ticket

- Ask students to reflect on the lesson and complete a short worksheet or exit ticket with the following prompts:
  - o   What is one new energy source you learned about today?
  - o   What are the benefits of using renewable energy sources?
  - o   How can you help conserve energy at home or school?

Adaptations for Diverse Learners:

- Provide additional resources or simplified articles on energy sources for students who need more support.
- Allow advanced learners to explore more complex energy solutions, such as energy-efficient technologies.
- Offer sentence starters for students who need assistance in forming their arguments during the group presentations.

Homework Extension:

Ask students to research a real-world energy project or an innovative solution to an energy problem (e.g., a community using solar energy, a wind farm, or energy-efficient homes). Students should prepare a short report or a presentation to share with the class.

Lesson Plan: Respiratory System - The Flipped Classroom Strategy

Grade Level: 6–8
Duration: 60 minutes
Theme: <u>Understanding the respiratory system using the flipped classroom strategy.</u>

Learning Objectives:

By the end of the lesson, students will be able to:

1. Understand the structure and function of the respiratory system.
2. Explain the process of breathing and gas exchange in the lungs.
3. Analyze how the respiratory system works with other body systems to maintain health.
4. Apply their knowledge through interactive activities and discussions.

Materials Needed:

*   Pre-recorded video explaining the respiratory system (covering its parts, functions, and process of breathing)
*   Printable worksheets with key vocabulary, diagrams of the respiratory system, and comprehension questions
*   Large chart paper and markers for group work
*   Access to a projector or smartboard for reviewing key concepts
*   Whiteboard for group discussion and reflections

Lesson Flow:

1. Engagement (5 minutes)
Activity: Introduction to the Lesson

- Start by asking students:
    - How do you think we breathe?
    - What body parts do you think are involved when we take a breath?
- Share with the class that they will be learning about the **respiratory system** today and how it helps our body get oxygen.
- Pose the inquiry question:
    - How does the respiratory system help us breathe and keep our body healthy?

2. Exploration (15 minutes)
Activity: Pre-Class Video Assignment (Flipped Classroom)

1. **Video Viewing:**
    - Before the class, assign students to watch a short video at home (or during the previous lesson if needed) that explains the respiratory system. The video should cover:
        - The main parts of the respiratory system (e.g., nose, trachea, lungs, diaphragm, alveoli).
        - The process of inhalation and exhalation.
        - How oxygen is exchanged for carbon dioxide in the lungs.
        - The role of the respiratory system in maintaining overall health.
2. **Worksheet:**
    - Provide students with a worksheet to complete while watching the video. The worksheet should include key vocabulary

(e.g., inhalation, exhalation, diaphragm, alveoli), a diagram to label, and a few comprehension questions to ensure understanding.
  - Ask students to bring their completed worksheets to class for the discussion.

3. Explanation (15 minutes)
Activity: In-Class Discussion and Group Work

1. **Class Review:**
   - Begin by reviewing the video content. Project a diagram of the respiratory system on the board and ask students to help label the parts.
   - Discuss the breathing process, focusing on how air travels into the body, through the trachea, into the lungs, and how gas exchange happens in the alveoli.
   - Clarify any misconceptions from the video or worksheet and answer any questions students may have.
2. **Group Activity:**
   - Divide the class into small groups (3–4 students per group).
   - Provide each group with a large piece of chart paper and markers. Ask them to create a visual representation of the respiratory system, including labeled parts and brief explanations of how each part functions.
   - Groups should include a section explaining how the respiratory system works with other systems, like the circulatory system.

4. Elaboration (15 minutes)
Activity: Collaborative Exploration

1. **Group Presentations**:
   - Have each group present their chart and explanation to the class. Encourage them to share what they learned about the respiratory system and how it helps our body.
2. **Interactive Questions**:
   - After each group's presentation, ask questions such as:
     - How does the respiratory system work with other systems in the body?
     - Why is it important to keep our respiratory system healthy?
     - How can things like smoking or pollution affect the respiratory system?
3. **Class Reflection**:
   - Use the whiteboard to summarize key points from the group presentations and class discussion.
   - Pose reflective questions to the class:
     - How would our body be affected if our respiratory system didn't work properly?
     - Can you think of any habits we can adopt to keep our respiratory system healthy?

5. Evaluation (5 minutes)
Activity: Exit Ticket or Reflection Sheet

- Give students an exit ticket or a reflection sheet with the following prompts:
  - What are the main parts of the respiratory system?
  - Why is the diaphragm important for breathing?

o   How does the respiratory system help keep your body healthy?
- Collect the tickets to gauge students' understanding of the topic.

Adaptations for Diverse Learners:

- Provide additional resources like simpler videos or graphic organizers for students who need extra support.
- Allow students to work in pairs or small groups during the video assignment if they need assistance with note-taking or understanding the content.
- For advanced learners, encourage them to explore more complex topics, such as how respiratory issues like asthma or bronchitis affect breathing.

Homework Extension:

Ask students to research one respiratory health problem (e.g., asthma, pneumonia) and prepare a short presentation or report that explains the condition and how it affects the respiratory system.

Lesson Plan: Exploring Adaptations in Animals – Think Aloud Protocol

Grade Level: 2–4
Duration: 60 minutes
Theme: <u>Understanding the adaptations in animals using think aloud protocol.</u>

Learning Objectives:

By the end of the lesson, students will be able to:

1. Define what adaptations are and how they help animals survive in their environments.
2. Identify different types of adaptations (physical and behavioral) in various animals.
3. Use the Think Aloud Protocol to demonstrate how they analyze and reason through scientific concepts.
4. Collaborate with peers to explore how animals adapt to specific environments.

Materials Needed:

- Images or videos of animals with different adaptations (e.g., a camel in the desert, a polar bear in the Arctic, a giraffe in the savannah)
- Chart paper and markers for group work
- Think Aloud Protocol worksheet (template with prompts to guide students through their thinking process)
- Whiteboard or smartboard for class discussion
- Examples of questions for guided thinking aloud

Lesson Flow:

1. Engagement (10 minutes)
Activity: Introduction to Adaptations

- Start by asking:
    - What do you think an adaptation is?
    - Can you think of any animals that have special features to help them survive in their environment?
- Write the responses on the board and briefly introduce the concept of adaptations:
    - **Adaptations** are special characteristics that help animals survive in their environment. These can be **physical** (body parts) or **behavioral** (ways of acting).
- Pose the inquiry question:
    - How do animals' adaptations help them survive in different environments?

2. Exploration (15 minutes)
Activity: Think Aloud Protocol Introduction

1. **Explain the Think Aloud Protocol**:
    - Tell students that they will practice thinking aloud, which means sharing their thought process as they work through a problem or question. This helps others understand how we reason through concepts.
2. **Model the Think Aloud Protocol**:
    - Show students how to "think aloud" by analyzing one animal's adaptation. For example, take the **camel**:
        - "When I think about camels, I know they live in the desert, which is very hot and dry. One important adaptation camels have is their

hump. I think the hump stores fat, which can be used for energy when food is scarce. This helps them survive in a place where food and water are hard to find."
  - o Write down the steps and reasoning on the board, explaining how the camel's physical adaptations help it survive in the desert.

3. **Group Activity Setup**:
    - o Divide students into small groups (3–4 students per group). Assign each group an animal to investigate (e.g., polar bear, giraffe, owl, fish, etc.).
    - o Provide each group with an image or video of their animal and a Think Aloud Protocol worksheet.

3. Explanation (15 minutes)
Activity: Group Exploration Using Think Aloud

1. **Group Work**:
    - o Ask each group to use the Think Aloud Protocol to analyze their animal's adaptations. Students should:
      - Identify physical and/or behavioral adaptations.
      - Think aloud as a group to explain why each adaptation is important for survival.
      - Discuss how the adaptations help the animal in its environment (e.g., the giraffe's long neck helps it reach high trees in the savannah).

2. **Monitor and Support**:
    - o Walk around the room to listen to groups thinking aloud and help guide their reasoning if needed.

4. Elaboration (10 minutes)
Activity: Group Presentations and Class Discussion

1. **Group Presentations:**
   - Have each group present their animal and share their "thinking aloud" process with the class. They should:
     - Describe the animal's environment.
     - Explain the adaptations and how they help the animal survive.
     - Share the group's thought process using the Think Aloud Protocol.
2. **Class Discussion:**
   - After each presentation, ask the class to think about how the adaptations discussed might be different in another environment (e.g., would a polar bear's thick fur work in the desert?).
   - Record key points and adaptations on the whiteboard or smartboard.

5. Evaluation (5 minutes)
Activity: Exit Ticket or Reflection

- Ask students to complete an exit ticket or reflection worksheet with the following prompts:
  - What is an example of a physical or behavioral adaptation you learned about today?
  - How do adaptations help animals survive in their environments?
  - How did the Think Aloud Protocol help you understand adaptations better?

Adaptations for Diverse Learners:

- Provide visual aids, such as diagrams or videos, to support understanding of adaptations.
- Allow students to work in pairs or small groups if they need help with the Think Aloud Protocol.
- Offer sentence starters for students who may struggle with expressing their thoughts aloud.
- For advanced learners, encourage them to investigate animals in extreme environments (e.g., deep sea creatures) and consider more complex adaptations.

Homework Extension:

Ask students to choose an animal that wasn't covered in class, research its adaptations, and write a short paragraph explaining how the animal's adaptations help it survive in its environment. Students should use the Think Aloud Protocol as a model for their writing.

Lesson Plan: Photosynthesis – Exit ticket strategy

Grade Level: 6–8
Duration: 60 minutes
Theme: Understanding the photosynthesis using the exit ticket strategy.

Learning Objectives

By the end of the lesson, students will:

1. Understand the process of photosynthesis and its importance to plants and other living organisms.
2. Identify the key components needed for photosynthesis (sunlight, water, carbon dioxide).
3. Use the Exit Ticket strategy to reflect on their understanding of photosynthesis and ask follow-up questions.

Materials Needed

- Diagram or chart showing the photosynthesis process.
- A live plant for demonstration.
- Flashcards with photosynthesis vocabulary (e.g., chlorophyll, oxygen, glucose).
- Worksheet with guided questions.
- Sticky notes or index cards for exit tickets.

Lesson Flow

1. Engage (10 minutes)

- **Warm-up Question**: Ask, "Why do you think plants are green? How do they get their food?"
- Show a short video or animation illustrating the process of photosynthesis.
- Prompt a quick discussion with questions like:
    - "What do you think plants need to grow?"
    - "How do you think they make their food?"

2. Explore (15 minutes)

- **Hands-on Demonstration**:
    - Show a live plant and explain its basic parts (leaves, stem, roots).
    - Use a flashlight to represent sunlight and a spray bottle to represent water, explaining how these help the plant grow.
- **Interactive Diagram**:
    - Display a labeled diagram of photosynthesis.
    - Explain the process step-by-step:
        1. Plants take in carbon dioxide from the air through their leaves.
        2. Roots absorb water from the soil.
        3. Chlorophyll in leaves captures sunlight.
        4. Plants produce glucose (food) and release oxygen as a byproduct.

3. Explain (15 minutes)

- **Key Vocabulary**: Introduce words like photosynthesis, chlorophyll, carbon dioxide, glucose, oxygen, and sunlight.
- **Group Activity**:
    - Divide the class into small groups.

o   Provide each group with flashcards or puzzles that depict steps of the photosynthesis process.
o   Groups arrange the cards in the correct sequence and discuss each step.

4. Elaborate (15 minutes)

- **Discussion Prompt**: Ask, "What would happen if plants couldn't do photosynthesis?"
- **Extension Activity**:
    o   Have students create a comic strip or draw a diagram showing how a plant makes its food.
    o   Discuss the importance of photosynthesis to animals and humans (e.g., providing oxygen, forming the base of food chains).

5. Evaluate with Exit Ticket Strategy (5 minutes)

- **Activity Steps**:
    o   Distribute sticky notes or index cards to each student.
    o   Ask students to write down:
        1. One thing they learned about photosynthesis.
        2. One question they still have.
    o   Collect the exit tickets as they leave the classroom.
- Use the responses to assess understanding and plan follow-up lessons to address any gaps or questions.

Extensions

- **Experiment**: Grow two plants, one exposed to sunlight and the other kept in the dark. Observe and discuss the differences over time.

- **Environmental Connection**: Discuss how deforestation affects the oxygen supply and how plants contribute to a balanced ecosystem.
- **STEM Integration**: Build a simple model of a leaf showing how sunlight, water, and carbon dioxide are absorbed.

Lesson Plan: Understanding Food Webs

Grade Level: 3–5
Duration: 60 minutes
Theme: <u>Understanding the food webs using the graphic organizer.</u>

Learning Objectives

By the end of the lesson, students will:

1. Understand the concept of food webs and how they represent relationships between organisms in an ecosystem.
2. Identify producers, consumers (herbivores, carnivores, omnivores), and decomposers.
3. Use graphic organizers to visually represent a food web.

Materials Needed

- Chart paper or digital board for visuals.
- Pictures or cards of various plants and animals.
- Graphic organizer templates (printed or hand-drawn).
- Markers, crayons, and scissors.
- Worksheet with reflective questions about food webs.

Lesson Flow

1. Engage (10 minutes)

- **Warm-up Question**: Ask, "What do animals eat to survive? How do plants get their energy?"
- Show a short video or a colorful image of a food web from a specific ecosystem (e.g., forest, ocean, grassland).
- Prompt discussion:
    - "What connections can you see between the plants and animals in this picture?"
    - "Why do you think these connections are important?"

2. Explore (15 minutes)

- **Hands-on Demonstration**:
    - Display pictures of plants, herbivores, carnivores, omnivores, and decomposers.
    - Arrange the pictures in a simple chain (e.g., grass → rabbit → fox → fungi) and explain how energy flows from one organism to the next.
- **Interactive Activity**:
    - Provide small groups with picture cards of various organisms.
    - Challenge them to arrange the cards into a basic food chain, identifying the producer, consumer, and decomposer.

3. Explain (10 minutes)

- **Introduction to Food Webs**:
    - Use a diagram to show how food chains interconnect to form a food web.
    - Explain key terms: producer, consumer (herbivore, carnivore, omnivore), decomposer, and energy flow.

- o Highlight the importance of balance in an ecosystem and what happens if one species is removed.
- **Discussion Questions**:
    - o "What happens if there are too many herbivores in an ecosystem?"
    - o "What role do decomposers play in keeping the environment clean?"

4. Elaborate with Graphic Organizers (20 minutes)

- **Strategy Introduction**: Explain that students will create their own food web using a graphic organizer.
- **Activity Steps**:
    1. Distribute templates with blank spaces for producers, consumers, and decomposers.
    2. Provide students with a list of plants and animals from a chosen ecosystem (e.g., rainforest, ocean, desert).
    3. Students draw or paste pictures of organisms into the organizer and use arrows to show energy flow.
    4. Label each organism as a producer, herbivore, carnivore, omnivore, or decomposer.
- **Sharing**:
    - o Students present their food webs to the class.
    - o Discuss similarities and differences in the food webs created by different groups.

5. Evaluate (5 minutes)

- **Reflection Worksheet**: Students answer questions such as:
    1. What is the role of producers in a food web?

2. Why are decomposers important?
3. What would happen if one part of the food web was removed?

- **Optional Peer Review**: Students exchange graphic organizers and provide one positive comment about their peer's work.

Extensions

- **Real-World Connection**: Discuss how human activities (e.g., deforestation, pollution) impact food webs.
- **Art Integration**: Create a large mural of a food web as a class project.
- **Technology Integration**: Use online tools or apps to create digital food webs.

Lesson Plan: Exploring States of Matter

Grade Level: 3–5
Duration: 60 minutes
Theme: <u>Understanding the states of matter using the learning stations strategy.</u>

Learning Objectives

By the end of the lesson, students will:

1. Identify the three main states of matter (solid, liquid, gas) and their properties.
2. Observe and describe how matter can change from one state to another (melting, freezing, evaporation, condensation).
3. Explore the states of matter through hands-on learning stations and collaborative inquiry.

Materials Needed

- Ice cubes, water, and a kettle or cup with warm water.
- Balloons (to demonstrate gases).
- Small solid objects (e.g., a rock, toy, eraser).
- Clear plastic cups, thermometers, and food coloring.
- Science journals or worksheets for observations.
- Station instruction cards.

Lesson Flow

1. Engage (10 minutes)

- **Warm-up Activity**:

- o   Display a mystery box containing an ice cube, a bottle of water, and an inflated balloon.
  - o   Ask, "What do these objects have in common? How are they different?"
  - o   Take student guesses and introduce the concept of solids, liquids, and gases as states of matter.
- **Discussion Question**: "What happens when ice melts or when water boils? Can you think of other examples of changes in matter?"

2. Explore (30 minutes)

Learning Stations Activity:

- **Strategy Overview**: Introduce the concept of learning stations, where students will work in small groups to explore states of matter through hands-on activities.
- Divide the class into 3–4 groups. Each group rotates through the following stations:

Station 1: Solid to Liquid (Melting)

- **Materials**: Ice cubes, clear plastic cups.
- **Activity**:
  - o   Students observe an ice cube melting in a cup at room temperature.
  - o   Record observations about how the solid changes into a liquid over time.
  - o   Discuss: "What causes the ice to melt?"

Station 2: Liquid to Gas (Evaporation)

- **Materials**: Warm water in a cup or bowl, kettle (optional), mirrors.

- **Activity**:
  - o Students observe steam rising from warm water or a kettle.
  - o Hold a mirror above the steam to collect condensation.
  - o Discuss: "What happens to the water as it heats up?"

Station 3: Gas in Action

- **Materials**: Balloons, air pump, and straws.
- **Activity**:
  - o Inflate balloons and observe their shape and movement when released.
  - o Discuss: "How do we know there is gas inside the balloon?"

Station 4: Changing Temperatures (Optional)

- **Materials**: Thermometers, water at different temperatures, food coloring.
- **Activity**:
  - o Add food coloring to cold and warm water and observe the movement of the color.
  - o Discuss: "How does temperature affect liquids?"

3. Explain (10 minutes)

- **Group Sharing**:
  - o After rotating through stations, groups share their observations and discuss what they learned at each station.
  - o Use a visual chart to consolidate information about the properties of solids, liquids, and gases.

- **Key Terms**: Introduce and reinforce vocabulary such as melting, freezing, evaporation, condensation, and states of matter.

4. Elaborate (5 minutes)

- **Real-Life Connections**:
    - Ask students to think of examples of state changes in their daily lives (e.g., popsicles melting, water boiling, dew forming on grass).
    - Discuss the importance of these processes in nature and everyday activities.

5. Evaluate with Science Journals (5 minutes)

- Students answer questions in their journals or worksheets:
    1. What are the three main states of matter?
    2. Describe one example of a solid changing into a liquid.
    3. What did you observe about gases at the stations?
- Collect journals to assess understanding and areas for follow-up.

Extensions

- **Experiment at Home**: Students can observe ice melting in different environments (e.g., sunlight vs. shade) and report their findings.
- **Art Integration**: Create a poster or drawing of the states of matter with labeled transitions (e.g., melting, freezing, evaporation).
- **STEM Challenge**: Design a container that can keep ice from melting for as long as possible.

Lesson Plan: Exploring Multiplication - Peer Teaching

Grade Level: 3–5
Duration: 60 minutes
Theme: <u>Solving Multiplication sums using peer teaching strategy.</u>

Learning Objectives

By the end of the lesson, students will:

1. Understand the concept of multiplication as repeated addition or grouping.
2. Solve basic multiplication problems using arrays, number lines, and word problems.
3. Develop confidence in teaching multiplication concepts to their peers.

Materials Needed

- Multiplication charts and flashcards.
- Manipulatives (e.g., counters, cubes, or buttons).
- Whiteboards and markers.
- Prepared worksheets with multiplication problems.
- Peer teaching guide handouts (with step-by-step examples).

Lesson Flow

1. Engage (10 minutes)

- **Warm-up Activity:**

- o Show a simple repeated addition problem (e.g., 4 + 4 + 4) and ask students, "Is there an easier way to solve this?"
  - o Introduce multiplication as repeated addition and give examples like:
    - $4 + 4 + 4 = 3 \times 4 = 12$
    - $5 + 5 + 5 + 5 = 4 \times 5 = 20$
- **Discussion Prompt**: "Where do we use multiplication in real life?" (e.g., counting groups, arrays, shopping).

2. Explore (15 minutes)

- **Hands-on Exploration**:
  - o Use counters or cubes to demonstrate multiplication:
    - Example: Arrange 3 groups of 4 counters and write the multiplication equation $3 \times 4 = 12$.
    - Ask students to create their own groups and equations with manipulatives.
- **Interactive Learning**:
  - o Solve a few problems as a class using number lines and arrays to reinforce understanding.

3. Explain (10 minutes)

- **Key Concept Breakdown**:
  - o Multiplication terms: factors, product.
  - o Multiplication strategies: repeated addition, arrays, skip counting.
  - o Provide examples on the board and solve them together.
- **Peer Teaching Preparation**:

- o   Pair up students and explain that each partner will take turns teaching a multiplication concept.
- o   Distribute peer teaching guides with step-by-step instructions and examples, such as:
    - ▪   Step 1: Show a problem using counters.
    - ▪   Step 2: Explain the equation and solve it.
    - ▪   Step 3: Ask the other student to try a similar problem.

4. Elaborate with Peer Teaching (20 minutes)

- **Activity Steps**:
    1. **Practice Teaching**: Each pair is given a set of multiplication problems.
        - ▪   Partner A teaches the concept of multiplication for the first problem while Partner B listens, asks questions, and solves the next example.
        - ▪   Switch roles for the next problem.
    2. **Challenge Problems**: Provide slightly more complex word problems for pairs to solve together, reinforcing their understanding and teaching skills.
- **Monitor and Support**:
    - o   Walk around the room to observe and provide guidance as needed.
    - o   Encourage students to explain their reasoning clearly and use multiple strategies when teaching.

5. Evaluate (5 minutes)

- **Quick Assessment**:

- o   Each student solves one multiplication problem independently on a whiteboard.
  - o   Share answers and discuss strategies used.
- **Reflection Question**: Ask, "What was the most helpful thing your partner taught you today?" and have students share their responses.

Extensions

- **Real-Life Connection**: Assign a task where students find and solve a multiplication problem from their daily life (e.g., counting total pencils in packs of 5).
- **Technology Integration**: Use multiplication apps or online games for practice.
- **Art Integration**: Create a "multiplication garden" by drawing arrays of flowers, grouping petals to represent equations.

Lesson Plan: Persuasive Writing - Quick Writes

Grade Level: 3–5
Duration: 60 minutes
Theme: <u>Understanding the persuasive writing using the quick writes strategy.</u>

Learning Objectives

By the end of the lesson, students will:

1. Understand the purpose and structure of persuasive writing.
2. Develop quick brainstorming and writing skills using the Quick Write strategy.
3. Create a persuasive paragraph expressing their opinion on a topic.

Materials Needed

- Chart paper or whiteboard for brainstorming.
- Persuasive writing graphic organizers.
- Timer or stopwatch for Quick Write sessions.
- Writing notebooks or lined paper.
- Examples of age-appropriate persuasive writing.

Lesson Flow

1. Engage (10 minutes)

- **Warm-up Activity**:
    - Pose a fun question to the class: "Which is better: Ice cream or pizza? Why?"

- o   Encourage students to share their opinions and reasons.
  - o   Write responses on the board to demonstrate how reasons support opinions.
- **Introduce Persuasive Writing**:
  - o   Explain that persuasive writing is used to convince someone to agree with your opinion.
  - o   Show an example of a persuasive paragraph with clear arguments (e.g., convincing someone to adopt a class pet or extend recess).

2. Explore (15 minutes)

- **Brainstorming Ideas**:
  - o   Present a few topics relevant to the students (e.g., "Should homework be banned?", "Which pet is better: cats or dogs?", "Why should we have more recess time?").
  - o   As a class, brainstorm reasons for and against one of the topics and write them on the board.
- **Interactive Discussion**:
  - o   Ask students, "Which of these reasons do you find most convincing? Why?"
  - o   Highlight how specific examples or experiences make arguments stronger.

3. Explain (10 minutes)

- **Structure of Persuasive Writing**:
  - o   Break down the components of a persuasive paragraph:
    1. **Opening Statement**: Clearly state your opinion.

2. **Reasons with Examples**: Provide 2–3 strong reasons with examples to support your opinion.
        3. **Closing Statement**: Restate your opinion and include a call to action (e.g., "That's why we should have more recess!").
- **Introduce Quick Writes**:
    - Explain that Quick Writes are short, timed writing activities to help brainstorm and organize thoughts quickly.
    - Model a Quick Write by writing a 2-minute response to the prompt: "Why is reading important?"

4. Elaborate with Quick Writes (20 minutes)

- **Activity Steps**:
    1. Present a prompt (e.g., "What is the best way to spend a school break?" or "Why should kids help with chores at home?").
    2. Set a timer for 3 minutes. Students write as many reasons and examples as possible without worrying about grammar or spelling.
    3. After time is up, students share their ideas with a partner or small group.
- **Drafting the Paragraph**:
    - Using their Quick Write ideas, students organize their thoughts into a persuasive paragraph using the structure provided earlier.
    - Remind them to include an opening statement, reasons with examples, and a closing statement.

5. Evaluate (5 minutes)

- **Peer Review**:
    - Students exchange paragraphs with a partner to review.
    - Encourage peers to check for:
        - A clear opinion in the opening statement.
        - At least two convincing reasons with examples.
        - A strong closing statement.
- **Reflection**:
    - Ask students to answer: "What did you enjoy about writing your opinion? What was challenging?"
    - Collect the paragraphs to assess understanding and provide feedback.

Extensions

- **Class Debate**: Turn the topics into a friendly debate where students present their persuasive arguments.
- **Art Integration**: Create posters to visually support their written arguments (e.g., drawing reasons why cats make better pets).
- **Real-Life Application**: Write a letter to the principal persuading them to make a change at school (e.g., adding a school garden or more library time).

Lesson Plan: Exploring Animal Habitats - Mind Mapping

Grade Level: 2–4
Duration: 60 minutes
Theme: <u>Understanding the animal habitats using the mind mapping strategy.</u>

Learning Objectives

By the end of the lesson, students will:

1. Identify various types of animal habitats and the animals that live there.
2. Understand the relationship between animals and their habitats, including adaptations.
3. Use mind mapping to organize and present information about habitats and their features.

Materials Needed

- Large chart paper or whiteboard for creating a class mind map.
- Colored markers and pencils.
- Individual mind mapping templates or blank sheets of paper.
- Reference books, images, or videos about animal habitats.
- Flashcards with examples of animals and their habitats.

Lesson Flow

1. Engage (10 minutes)

- **Warm-up Activity**:
    - Show pictures or short video clips of various habitats (e.g., desert, rainforest, ocean, grassland, arctic).
    - Ask:
        - "What do you notice about these places?"
        - "Which animals do you think live here and why?"
    - Write students' responses on the board to build curiosity.
- **Discussion Prompt**:
    - Ask students, "What do animals need to survive in their habitats?"
    - Highlight key factors like food, water, shelter, and climate.

2. Explore (15 minutes)

- **Group Activity**:
    - Divide students into small groups and assign each group a habitat (e.g., desert, rainforest, ocean, grassland, arctic).
    - Provide flashcards or images of animals and ask groups to match the animals to their habitats.
- **Guided Inquiry**:
    - Encourage groups to think about:
        - "Why does this animal live in this habitat?"
        - "How does it adapt to survive here?"

3. Explain (10 minutes)

- **Introduce Mind Mapping**:

- o Show a sample mind map on the board with a central idea (e.g., "Rainforest"). Branches should include:
    - Types of animals (e.g., monkeys, jaguars, parrots).
    - Features of the habitat (e.g., trees, heavy rainfall, warm temperatures).
    - Adaptations (e.g., monkeys use trees to move, parrots have strong beaks for nuts).
- **Model the Process**:
  - o Create a simple class mind map for a habitat (e.g., desert) while thinking aloud:
    - Central idea: Desert.
    - Branches: Animals, features (sand, hot), adaptations (camels store water).

4. Elaborate with Mind Mapping (20 minutes)

- **Individual/Group Activity**:
  1. Provide each student or group with a blank sheet or a template for creating a mind map.
  2. Assign or let them choose a habitat to explore further.
  3. Students draw the central idea (habitat name) and add branches:
     - Animals found there.
     - Habitat features (climate, vegetation, etc.).
     - Adaptations of animals.
  4. Encourage them to use drawings, colors, and labels for creativity.
- **Sharing and Discussion**:
  - o Have students present their mind maps to the class.

- o Encourage peer questions and feedback.

5. Evaluate (5 minutes)

- **Quick Assessment**:
    - o Ask students to write one thing they learned about a specific habitat and one question they still have.
    - o Review their mind maps for completeness and creativity.
- **Reflection Question**:
    - o "Why do you think it's important to understand animal habitats and adaptations?"

Extensions

- **Research Project**: Students choose an endangered animal and create a mind map about its habitat, threats, and how to protect it.
- **STEAM Integration**: Build a 3D model of a chosen habitat using recycled materials.
- **Creative Writing**: Write a story from the perspective of an animal describing its habitat and daily life.

Lesson Plan: Understanding the Importance of Rules Through Socratic Seminars

Grade Level: 1–3
Duration: 60 minutes
Theme: Understanding the importance of rules and regulations using the Socratic seminars.

Learning Objectives

By the end of the lesson, students will:

1. Understand why rules are necessary in various contexts (e.g., classroom, home, society).
2. Develop critical thinking and listening skills by participating in a Socratic Seminar.
3. Articulate and defend their opinions about the importance of rules.

Materials Needed

- Chart paper or whiteboard for note-taking.
- Prepared questions for the Socratic Seminar (e.g., "What would happen if there were no rules in the classroom?").
- Copies of a short story or article about rules (e.g., "The Day Everyone Broke the Rules").
- Student response journals or notebooks.
- A talking stick or object to signify who is speaking.

Lesson Flow

1. Engage (10 minutes)

- **Warm-up Activity**:
  - o Present a scenario: "Imagine you came to school, and there were no rules. What do you think would happen?"
  - o Ask students to share their thoughts while you note key points on the board.
  - o Discuss the role of rules in creating order, safety, and fairness.
- **Introduce Key Question**:
  - o Pose the central question for the lesson: "Why are rules important in our lives?"

2. Explore (15 minutes)

- **Reading or Story Activity**:
  - o Read a short story or article about rules, such as "The Day Everyone Broke the Rules."
  - o After reading, discuss:
    - ▪ "What happened when the rules were broken?"
    - ▪ "What do you think the author is trying to teach us?"
- **Brainstorming Session**:
  - o As a class, brainstorm examples of rules at school, home, and in the community.
  - o Group similar ideas under categories (e.g., safety rules, fairness rules).

3. Explain (10 minutes)

Introduce the Socratic Seminar:
- o Explain that students will participate in a structured discussion to share their ideas about the importance of rules.
  - o Emphasize the rules of the seminar:
    - ▪ Listen respectfully to others.

- Speak one at a time and stay on topic.
            - Use evidence or examples to support your opinion.
- **Model the Process**:
    - Demonstrate how to answer a question thoughtfully and build on others' ideas. For example:
        - Question: "Are all rules fair?"
        - Example Response: "I think some rules are fair because they keep us safe, like stop signs. But others might seem unfair, like not being allowed to chew gum in school. Maybe they have reasons we don't understand."

4. Elaborate with Socratic Seminar (20 minutes)

- **Discussion Questions**:
    1. "What would happen if there were no rules in our school or community?"
    2. "Are all rules necessary? Why or why not?"
    3. "Who decides what rules are important?"
    4. "Can rules ever be changed? Give an example."
- **Facilitating the Seminar**:
    - Seat students in a circle and use a talking stick to ensure only one person speaks at a time.
    - Guide the discussion with follow-up questions or prompts, such as:
        - "Can you give an example to support your opinion?"
        - "Do you agree or disagree with what was just said?"

-

- **Teacher Role**:
    - o   Act as a facilitator, ensuring all voices are heard and keeping the discussion on track.

5. Evaluate (5 minutes)

- **Reflection Activity**:
    - o   Ask students to write a short journal entry answering:
        - ▪   "What did I learn about the importance of rules today?"
        - ▪   "Did someone say something in the discussion that changed my mind? Why?"
- **Peer Feedback**:
    - o   Have students share one thing they learned from a classmate during the seminar.

Extensions

- **Research Project**: Assign students to research a specific rule (e.g., traffic laws or school rules) and explain its purpose and impact.
- **Creative Writing**: Have students write a fictional story about a day without rules in their favorite place.
- **Art Integration**: Create posters highlighting important rules and their benefits (e.g., "Stay Safe by Following Traffic Lights").

Lesson Plan: Exploring the Impact of Technology on Communication - Case Studies

Grade Level: 6–8
Duration: 60 minutes
Theme: Understanding the impact of technology on communication using the case studies strategy.

Learning Objectives

By the end of the lesson, students will:

1. Identify different ways people communicate with and without technology.
2. Analyze case studies to understand the impact of technology on communication.
3. Discuss the positive and negative effects of technology on how we connect with others.

Materials Needed

- Printed or digital copies of case studies (e.g., "A Day Without a Smartphone," "Pen Pals Then and Now").
- Chart paper or whiteboard for collaborative brainstorming.
- Markers or pens for group work.
- Writing notebooks or response sheets for reflections.
- Access to visuals or videos illustrating traditional and modern communication methods.

Lesson Flow

1. Engage (10 minutes)

- **Warm-up Activity**:
    - o   Ask students, "How do you talk to your friends or family members who live far away?"
    - o   Write responses on the board (e.g., phone calls, texts, emails, video calls, letters).
- **Discussion Prompt**:
    - o   Pose the question: "How do you think people communicated before phones or computers existed?"
    - o   Show visuals or a short video comparing traditional (letters, in-person) and modern (texts, emails) communication.
- **Introduce the Topic**:
    - o   Explain that technology has changed the way we communicate, and today they will explore how this impacts our lives.

2. Explore (15 minutes)

- **Introduce Case Studies**:
    - o   Explain that they will read real-life or fictional scenarios (case studies) about communication with and without technology.
    - o   Distribute case studies to small groups. Examples:
        1. "A Day Without a Smartphone" (A student forgets their phone at home and must find ways to communicate).
        2. "Pen Pals Then and Now" (A story comparing how pen pals communicated through letters in the past versus emails today).
- **Guided Group Work**:

- o   In groups, students read their assigned case study and discuss:
    - "What was the main way people communicated in this story?"
    - "What challenges did they face?"
    - "How did technology help or complicate communication?"

3. Explain (10 minutes)

- **Facilitating Class Discussion**:
    - o   Have groups share their case study summaries and insights with the class.
    - o   Use guiding questions:
        - "What would you have done in this situation?"
        - "Do you think technology made communication better or harder in this story?"
- **Highlight Key Points**:
    - o   Create a two-column chart titled "Impact of Technology on Communication" with Positive and Negative sides.
    - o   Fill in student responses (e.g., Positive: faster messages, video calls; Negative: distractions, less face-to-face time).

4. Elaborate with Case Study Analysis (20 minutes)

- **Activity Steps**:
    1. Assign a new case study or create hypothetical ones (e.g., "Using Only Letters for a Week").
    2. Groups answer deeper questions about their case:
        - "What problems could arise from using only traditional methods?"

- ▪ "What are the risks of relying only on technology?"
    3. Groups create a small presentation (poster, skit, or summary) to illustrate their analysis.
- **Sharing and Reflection**:
    - o Each group presents their findings.
    - o Encourage peer questions and discussion.

5. Evaluate (5 minutes)

- **Exit Ticket Activity**:
    - o Ask students to write or discuss:
        - ▪ "One way technology has improved communication."
        - ▪ "One challenge technology has created for communication."
- **Class Reflection**:
    - o Summarize the lesson by revisiting the chart and emphasizing balance: "Technology can help us, but we also need to communicate face-to-face sometimes."

Extensions

- **Research Project**:
    - o Students research and compare a historical communication method (e.g., telegraphs or letters) with a modern one (e.g., email or social media).
- **Creative Writing**:
    - o Write a short story imagining life without any modern technology for communication.
- **Debate**:
    - o Host a class debate on the topic: "Is technology making communication better or worse?"

Lesson Plan: Enhancing Narrative Writing - Reflection Circles

Grade Level: 4–6
Duration: 60 minutes
Theme: <u>Enhancing the narrative writing using the reflection circle strategy.</u>

Learning Objectives

By the end of the lesson, students will:

1. Understand the key elements of a narrative (characters, setting, problem, solution, and sequence).
2. Use reflection circles to evaluate their own and others' narrative writing.
3. Provide and receive constructive feedback to improve their narratives.

Materials Needed

- Writing notebooks or drafts of students' narrative pieces.
- Reflection prompts (e.g., "What did you like about the story?" "What could be improved?").
- Chart paper or whiteboard to record group insights.
- Colored sticky notes or index cards for feedback.

Lesson Flow

1. Engage (10 minutes)
- **Warm-up Activity**
  o Ask students: "What makes a great story?"

- o Write their responses on the board, categorizing them under headings like Characters, Setting, Plot, etc.
  - o Show an example of a short narrative and highlight its elements.
- **Discussion Prompt**:
  - o Pose the question: "Why is it important to reflect on our writing?"
  - o Introduce the concept of reflection circles as a way to improve writing through shared feedback.

2. Explore (15 minutes)

- **Mini-Lesson on Narrative Writing**:
  - o Review the essential components of a narrative:
    - Characters
    - Setting
    - Problem
    - Solution
    - Sequence of events
  - o Share a short sample narrative and discuss how these elements appear in the story.
- **Model Reflection**:
  - o Read the sample story aloud and model reflective thinking:
    - "I really liked how the author described the setting—it felt like I was there!"
    - "I think the ending could be stronger by showing how the character solved the problem."

3. Explain (10 minutes)

- **Introduce Reflection Circles**:

- o Explain the process:
  1. Students will share their narratives in small groups.
  2. Group members will take turns giving feedback using prompts:
     - "What part of the story stood out to you?"
     - "Was there a part that confused you?"
     - "What suggestion do you have to make the story even better?"
- o Emphasize the importance of respectful, constructive feedback.
- **Feedback Guidelines**:
  - o Teach the "Glow and Grow" method:
    - Glow: One thing the writer did well.
    - Grow: One thing that could be improved.

4. Elaborate with Reflection Circles (20 minutes)

- **Activity Steps**:
  1. Divide students into groups of 4–5.
  2. Each student shares their narrative with the group, either reading it aloud or summarizing it.
  3. Group members take turns providing feedback using the reflection prompts.
  4. Writers jot down notes on what they learned from the feedback.
- **Teacher's Role**:
  - o Move between groups to facilitate discussions and ensure all students are participating.

5. Evaluate (5 minutes)

- **Individual Reflection**:
    - Ask students to answer the following in their notebooks:
        - "What feedback did I receive?"
        - "What will I change in my story based on the feedback?"
- **Class Sharing**:
    - Invite a few volunteers to share one piece of feedback they received and how it will improve their writing.

Extensions

- **Editing Workshop**:
    - After revisions, have students swap stories with a peer for a final round of feedback.
- **Publishing Opportunity**:
    - Create a class anthology of revised narratives and share it with parents or other classes.
- **Art Integration**:
    - Illustrate a scene from their narrative to accompany their final draft.

Lesson Plan: Mastering Subtraction - Think-Show-Apply Strategy

Grade Level: 1–3
Duration: 60 minutes
Theme: Enhancing Subtraction Skills Using Think-Show-Apply

Learning Objectives

By the end of the lesson, students will:

1. Understand the concept and process of subtraction.
2. Use visual representations to solve subtraction problems.
3. Apply subtraction skills to real-world problems through hands-on activities.

Materials Needed

- Whiteboard or chart paper for demonstrations.
- Number cards or counters for hands-on activities.
- Worksheets with subtraction problems (e.g., simple, multi-digit).
- Visual aids (e.g., pictures or diagrams for story problems).
- Sticky notes or index cards for group reflection.

Lesson Flow

1. Engage (10 minutes)

- **Warm-up Activity:**
    - Ask: "What do you think subtraction is?"
    - Write student responses on the board and build a definition together: "Subtraction is

taking away or finding the difference between two numbers."

- o Show a simple subtraction example, like 10 − 4 = ?, and ask students to think about how they would solve it.

- **Discussion Prompt**:
  - o Pose the question: "When would you need to subtract in real life?"
  - o Provide examples such as: shopping, counting down days, and sharing items.

2. Explore (15 minutes)

- **Introduce Think-Show-Apply**:
  - o **Think**: Present a subtraction problem (e.g., 15 − 7 = ?). Ask students to think about how they might approach solving it.
  - o **Show**: Demonstrate the solution on the board using visual aids such as counters, number lines, or drawings. Show how to count backward or use groupings to subtract.
    - Example:
      - 15 − 7 = ?
      - Start with 15 counters and remove 7, showing how the remaining counters equal 8.
  - o **Apply**: Give students a similar problem to solve independently using counters, number lines, or drawings.

3. Explain (10 minutes)

- **Review Subtraction Strategies**:
  - o Introduce different subtraction methods (e.g., counting backward, using number

lines, decomposing numbers) and highlight when each strategy is most helpful.

- o **Example**:
    - For 15 – 7 = ?, students can think of it as 10 – 7 = 3 and then add back the remaining 5 to get the final answer.
- o Show how subtraction can be used to solve word problems. For example:
    - "Sarah has 15 apples. She gives 7 to her friend. How many apples does she have left?"
    - Write the problem on the board and model solving it step by step using the Think-Show-Apply method.

4. Elaborate with Hands-On Practice (20 minutes)

- **Activity Steps**:
    1. **Think**: Present students with a real-world subtraction problem (e.g., You have 24 marbles. You give 8 marbles away. How many marbles do you have left?).
    2. **Show**: Ask students to draw a picture, use counters, or use a number line to represent the problem visually.
    3. **Apply**: Have students solve similar problems individually or in pairs. Provide worksheets with varying levels of difficulty, including both simple and word problems.
- **Group Work**:
    - o In pairs, students can create their own subtraction word problems and swap them with another pair to solve. Encourage them to apply subtraction strategies discussed.

5. Evaluate (5 minutes)

- **Reflection**:
    - Ask students to share how they solved one of their problems and which method worked best for them.
    - Write key insights on the board about the strategies students used (e.g., "I used a number line to subtract" or "I drew pictures to help me visualize").
- **Exit Ticket**:
    - Give each student an exit ticket with one subtraction problem and ask them to write down the method they used to solve it.

Extensions

- **Challenge Problems:**
    - For advanced students, provide problems involving larger numbers or multi-step subtraction.
- **Subtraction Games:**
    - Create a subtraction bingo game or digital games that help reinforce subtraction skills in a fun way.
- **Cross-Curricular Integration:**
    - Use subtraction in science or social studies contexts (e.g., calculating how much more food is needed for a group or how many days are left until an event).

Thank you for choosing to read **The Educator's Playbook.** Your time and dedication means so much. This book was created with a vision to support educators like you in crafting lessons that inspire curiosity, foster creativity, and make a lasting impact on students' lives. I am sure you will be surprise to draft amazing lessons and innovate new techniques after reading this book.

A special Thanks to **Rakhee Chhabria from Tealchershelpteachers**, who encouraged me to complete this book and turn my raw data and experience into something that will help others in making that impact.